NAVIGATING THE ART WORLD
Professional Practice for the Early Career Artist

DELPHIAN

ISBN
978-1-9997990-4-5

INTRODUCTION

We formed Delphian in 2016, born out of a mutual devotion to our artistic practices and love of curation. We see the art of curation as a creative act in itself, and one that would allow us an opportunity to support and encourage some of the amazing artists that we were discovering.

The meteoric rise of social media has done two things to the art world. Firstly, it has made it easier and cheaper for artists to share their work with the world. Secondly, it has made it easier for supporters and collectors to communicate directly with the artists whose work they love. This is a resolutely positive thing for artists, but it has made it harder than ever to run a gallery.

To survive, the majority of galleries need to sell artworks, but with social media allowing a closer connection between these collectors and the artists themselves, this has become increasingly difficult.

For this reason, we decided to take a slightly different approach. When we promote works online by artists represented by other galleries, we are directing our followers (and thus, potential buyers) to galleries other than ourselves. However, to understand this primarily as a "lost sale" is to take an overly reductive approach. Instead, we view this process as cyclical, and the more we help people discover great work – wherever this may be – the more they will keep coming back to us.

We don't see ourselves as a gallery in the typical sense – rather, we aspire to be *connectors*.

We believe that the more we share great work, the better off we'll all be, which is why we regularly help promote artists and shows at other galleries, regardless of whether or not these galleries return the favour.

It has been our intention to write about things that are not often discussed, in the hope that by pulling back the curtain slightly, things are a little clearer for all of us. We wanted this book to be as honest and as candid as possible, whilst also accepting the fact that we don't know everything. We have written these opinion-pieces with the aim of sharing some of the things we have learnt along the way.

With that in mind, it is important for us to convey one fact more than any other: there is no one path to success in life, and this is especially true in the arts. Some of what you read in these pages may not be entirely applicable to you, and some you may disagree with. This is entirely natural, and one of the most salient pieces of advice we could give would be this: seek out critique and advice from as many different sources as possible, and from sources that contradict each other. Consider all of this, and then decide what to use, and as importantly, what to ignore.

BENJAMIN MURPHY
NICK JS THOMPSON

FOREWORD: ON BEING A BUSINESS

Achieving any kind of success in the art world depends on two things: making interesting art (that goes without saying), and being good enough at getting that work out there. These two essential elements of an artist's practice could be referred to as the *Creative Side* and the *Business Side*, and both are as important as each other.

Many artists have a romantic idea of the profession; one centred around an almost complete rejection of the business practices that sustain the work. Unfortunately, this conception of an artist's profession is one better suited to the fantasy of film and literature than it is to actually making a living. Some galleries sign artists straight out of art school, but this is vanishingly uncommon and not something the vast majority of artists should be banking on. Galleries want to see a proven trajectory in an artist's career before they are going to invest time and money into supporting them. They often do a lot of careful research before even thinking of visiting an artist's studio, and so as an early career artist, it is your responsibility to make your work discoverable.

The first part of this journey is identifying that no-one is going to do all of this admin for you.

Managing admin is not what anyone, least of all artists, want to be dealing with. However, the sooner artists wake up to this reality the sooner they will begin to see the progression in both their career and in the work itself.

Social media is, for better or worse, something that we simply *have* to dedicate a substantial portion of this book to. This is because social media is now a huge part of how artists present their works to the world, and a huge part of how we, as both galleries and fans, discover art that we then go and seek-out in the flesh. Whilst social media definitely has its downsides, it is also an incredibly useful tool that far too many artists neglect at their peril.

In the vast majority of cases, what is seen on your social media will be the first impression people get of your work. If this isn't the case, then upon discovering your work elsewhere, most people go immediately to your social media to learn more about you. Where a well-designed website was once the most important way to deliver further information about yourself and your practice, now your social media has filled this role. Social media is dynamic where a website tends to be static, and as such people don't look to the latter for regular updates. Social media is fluid and ever-changing, so when done well, can keep yourself and your work fresh in people's minds.

If you are one of those artists who neglect social media on the basis of "just not being good at it", you are only disadvantaging yourself.

If you plan to sustain yourself working as a professional artist the first thing you need to do is start thinking of yourselves as a business. Once you do so, it becomes clear that there are areas beyond the making of art that require real, concentrated attention.

It takes time, and it takes practice. But our aim here is to try and bridge a small part of that gap between what you make and how you forge a career with it.

This book is a compendium of all the things we as practitioners have learned - often through trial and error, experimentation, jumping in at the deep end, and sometimes, simply winging it.

EMERGING SLOWLY

As an emerging artist, it can be disheartening to see your contemporaries succeed at what seems like a faster rate than yourself. This is a common feeling and widely shared within the artist community.

As is the case with most artists, a career is built in increments. Each show gradually builds on the last, in the same way as each work is the product of those that came before it. Overnight successes do happen, but they are by far the exception and not the rule. With no gradual trajectory, these few overnight successes are more vulnerable to instability and "fad" categorisation, leaving them susceptible to abandonment with the introduction of another hot new artist.

It can be much harder to maintain a career after such meteoric early success, as to progress you must keep building upon and diverging slightly from what went before. Without the proven track record of steady career progression, slight evolutions in practice, medium, or output can be alienating for new fans. The body of work that drew these new supporters to your practice might not necessarily speak of your work in general - and might not keep them in your corner once your work evolves again.

For this reason, artists should aim for their careers to progress at a steady rate rather than in fits and starts.

Whilst it is essential that all artists are perfectionists, this can be troublesome when coupled with a career that is sometimes deemed successful or otherwise based upon the approval of others.

As well as being perfectionists, artists are their own biggest critics. This is a good thing, but it is important to realise that as well as being your own worst critic, you must also be your own biggest champion - even when it might feel like your career has plateaued.

It is inevitable that some months will be more successful than others, be that in business or in making work, and so there will naturally be times when you feel like you are not progressing at the rate you should be (or have been). This issue is exacerbated when you compare yourselves with your contemporaries. So stop comparing.

That is to say, you should indeed be competitive, but only with yourself.

The beauty of being an emerging artist, and of not emerging too soon, is that you are afforded the freedom to experiment. You are able to explore the art world and your practice much more freely than a more established artist can, as they have responsibilities and deadlines that constrict their artistic freedom.

As an emerging artist you should cherish this time that allows you to develop and nurture your work in a way that is not derailed by overnight success. Often this overnight success dictates an artist's entire career, and they are left to play a constant and unbeatable game of catch-up. It can also force an artist to raise their prices quickly, which results in the artist having to drop their prices after the hysteria fades, or resign themselves to never selling again.

Another issue with becoming an 'established' artist too soon is that without the freedom to experiment, it is possible that this success can lead to the dilution of what makes one's work so exciting. While offering a certain amount of security, being established brings its own set of concerns; so for now, relax in your current position, whatever that may be.

Instead of chasing instant recognition, work hard, and have faith that your time will come.

HOW DO YOU FIND YOUR INSPIRATION?

ANDY DIXON

I can't turn the part of my brain off that mines for inspiration to be honest. Be it the colour of someone's shoes, the curved line of a tunnel, a pattern on a rug, or a leaf of a plant – I can't help but be constantly indexing sensory information into "good" or "bad" piles – both are equally inspiring

HAYDEN KAYS

Everything already exists, it's just a case of moving it about a little. Move it your own way, and call yourself an artist

MATTHEW ALLEN
I ascribe to Richard Serra's statement that "Work comes from work" – meaning that the impulse to continue and explore emerges from what has come before. My practice is an evolving feedback loop of material potentials and process-based responses

RAE HICKS
Coffee, and a decent length train journey

JUSTIN LEE WILLIAMS
I find it mostly in being on my own, building cabins in the woods or talking with odd and strange people. Hardly ever do I find it in art itself – that part is more just a channel for the craft

DANNY ROMERIL

Everyday life, art books, talking to people, things that happen, anything and everything. Nothing is safe. Not even tables

WRITER'S BLOCK

Being creative is a difficult endeavour, and it's one of the many reasons that some people struggle when it comes to being a full-time artist. For those that do manage it, often they can find themselves with a show or commission deadline looming, utterly unable to work. If the creativity isn't flowing, it just isn't flowing, and there is nothing you can do to force it. It can sometimes take days or weeks to get out of this creative slump, regardless of how much one might try.

It's best to avoid spending valuable time forcing your way through something when it isn't coming naturally. Instead, identify the inability to focus and move on. Use this time productively and return to your creative practice when you are better-suited to give it your best.

Wherever possible, it is always best to let this re-emergence happen organically, as any work forced out in one of these slow periods will often be your weakest. That's not to say that we shouldn't work during these times, but rather that we should focus on less concentration-heavy tasks until we are feeling ready to produce creatively once again. These times of sparse inspiration are also a great opportunity to do things like admin, prepare materials, or organise your studio space.

As outlined elsewhere in this book, the less exciting admin side of being an artist is as important as the creation of work, so use these breaks from creation to continue building your career, albeit in a different way.

The idea of *deep work* is one that recognises we only really do our best work a fraction of time that we actually spend working - and it is this deep, concentrated type of work that produces the best results. There are different variations of *deep work*; from *monastic* (that lasts for a long time), to *journalistic* (that lasts minutes or hours). Let these periods of deep concentration come when they will, and allow yourself the freedom to be unproductive when you are unable to force productivity. When experiencing writers' block switch between tasks often, as a refreshed mind is always better than a tired one.

Try to identify when you experience these states of deep concentration, and note down the conditions in which they came so that you can adjust your working environment to one in which these states are more common.

Procrastination is fine in moderation as the brain needs periods of rest occasionally (or it simply wouldn't seek them out). Wherever possible, allow these periods of rest to happen when they do, and come back to your work refreshed when you are able.

The American painter Chuck Close once said "Inspiration is for amateurs. The rest of us just show up and get to work. If you wait around for the clouds to part and a bolt of lightning to strike you in the brain, you are not going to make an awful lot of work. All the best ideas come out of the process; they come out of the work itself".

Whilst we often don't have the luxury of simply downing tools and taking the day off, what we can do is refocus our minds on a different thing from our to-do list. It's important to acknowledge the fact that we all inevitably sometimes hit periods of writers' block, and that is ok.

Jumping to another less creative task can be a good approach if you want to continue working, but if that doesn't work it is also fine to allow yourself the space and time to simply contemplate your next move, or to do something else entirely.

WHAT CAN ARTISTS DO TO GET THEIR WORK NOTICED?

GALERIE CHLOE SALGADO
Group shows and self-promotion on Instagram

MAUREEN PALEY
Present work on their own terms in self-made or indie venues

GALLERY STEINSLAND BERLINER
Keep on making it

NO GALLERY
Become part of their scene with the intention of adding to it, rather than some selfish hidden agenda

CHARLIE MILLS OF COLLECTIVE ENDING, BOLD TENDENCIES, AND HANNAH BARRY GALLERY

Have a website that is actually legible

KRISTIN HJELLEGJERDE GALLERY

Get together with other artists they admire in the same situation and do pop-up shows

WILLIAM GUSTAFSSON OF UNION GALLERY

Don't focus on getting representation – build your CV with shows, whether it's in a gallery or your living room

BUILDING YOUR PROFILE

Rosalind Davis

Rosalind Davis is an artist, curator, educator, and writer. With Annabel Tilley she co-wrote "What they didn't teach you in art school: What you need to know to survive as an artist". We asked her to draw on her knowledge and expertise to give us some of her top tips on how to build your profile as an artist.

- It is hugely important for artists to build their profile, networks and relationships, researching curators, galleries, press, and importantly other artists.

- You have to get your work out there, so seize opportunities and make the most of them; go the extra mile, be organised, professional, memorable, and present. Market your exhibitions, turn up to all of the events that may be happening through the run of an exhibition, and make time to invite and bring people to see the work outside of the private view. Don't just rely on others to do this for you.

- Create opportunities for yourself – you could create your own residency or curate your own exhibition. These are proactive and empowering things to do as an artist.

- Create a mailing list from visitors at your exhibitions or online mailing list sign-ups and then send out invitations to your subsequent exhibitions. People in the arts want to know you are active, progressing, dedicated, and professional. You're unlikely to get interest in your work if you don't tell people about it in some way.

- Ensure you give people enough notice about your exhibitions. Telling people about it on the day, or the night before is unprofessional.

- Make sure you have a visual business card ready for when you do meet people – these are powerful ways to connect with individuals in an over-saturated digital world. Anyone you meet that is of interest to you, follow-up with an email and use social media to connect.

- Spend time on writing and developing your artist's statement, or get someone to help you write it. Curators and collectors research artists and read around their work before inviting them to be in shows. An artist's statement can be a deal-breaker on whether you might be selected for an opportunity.

LOCATING AN AUDIENCE

Many artists find the process of showing their work to the world a difficult one, and their work failing to stir up public excitement can exacerbate that anxiety.

If you are struggling to find an audience, it's likely the result of one of three factors.

IT ISN'T ORIGINAL

A common question that we get asked increasingly often refers to one's 'individual style': more specifically, how to get to the point that your work is characteristically and identifiably, yours.

The first of these three factors is perhaps the most difficult to get right, as originality is not exactly easy to come by. However, there are things that you can do to allow yourself the freedom to grow into your practice, and once you have fully accepted this freedom, originality follows.

Many artists fall into the same traps in the formative stages of their careers, and unintentionally make derivative work that emulates whatever style of work it is they are interested in at that given time. We are asked "how do you create your signature style?" all the time, and the answer can only ever be, that artists need to find their signature styles, rather than create them.

The way in which artists discover their individuality takes time. Artists need to allow themselves the space and the freedom to experiment, exploring as many different mediums, subject matters, and approaches as possible. It is only through the process that artists develop this originality, as they slide subconsciously into repetitive patterns that build upon one another and form natural habits.

Originality is the accumulation of a series of these subconscious processes, that when seen as a whole, are a representation of the originality inherent in each individual. No two people are the same, and so it follows that no two people's work is the same. When one artist makes work that appears similar to another's, it either isn't as similar as it may appear, or someone isn't being true to their own individuality.

Another thing that can help artists encourage this budding individuality is to take in as much art as possible, from as many different approaches as possible. If your only reference material is Cubist painting, it is easy to see how the work you make might quickly become a reworking of Cubist paintings. When you absorb a vast array of different approaches to making, some will filter their way into your work, distilled through the prism of your personality. So give your mind as much inspiration as possible, from as many varying sources. Even seek out work that you dislike. It all helps.

IT ISN'T CONSIDERED

This issue is the easiest one to remedy, as all it relies upon is introspection and honest, objective self-critique.

Many early-career artists make works that either don't say the things that the creator intends them to say, or they fall short in some more tactile way (like being poorly-executed). To make a well-considered piece of work requires an artist to spend a lot of time ruminating upon how well-articulated a work is, and if they allow work out into the world that isn't doing what they intended it to do, the public will realise this laxity.

It is hard to be a perfectionist, whilst also allowing yourself to put out work that you could (given an infinite time to resolve) perfect. Never should an artist make a piece that they deem to be entirely perfect, as to have achieved perfection is to either display an undeserved hubris, or to lie to oneself. To deem a work perfect is to decide that it could never be improved, and to decide this is to stagnate.

The way to overcome this common pitfall is simple – seek out critique from as many different sources as possible, find people who won't simply flatter you, and encourage them to be as harsh as they think necessary when appraising your work. Collect as much of this critique as possible, hear it objectively, and try to learn from it. It may be the case that a lot of what you receive back is irrelevant or unimportant, but some of what you receive may just be the missing piece of the puzzle, and allow you to polish off an as-yet unpolished work.

Seek out critique rather than praise, but remember, one mustn't heed all of it all of the time.

IT ISN'T DISCOVERABLE

This is also a fairly easy thing to remedy, if your work is struggling to find an audience, you should re-evaluate how it is that you are sharing it with the world.

There are countless numbers of creatives out there, making their work and sharing it with the wider public in some way or other. This naturally means that there is more competition but it also means that there is more opportunity. If what you make is not gaining any traction, and you are confident that the other two aforementioned issues have been resolved, it is likely that you are simply placing your work in the wrong setting for the work itself.

It is important to know your audience, and to place your work in the right setting. This is not only so as to find the right people who will like your work, but it also allows it to be seen in its best light.

Seek out galleries and platforms that already attract an audience that might be interested in the kind of thing you're making. Think about style, context, and content, and look for places your work wouldn't look out of place. Just because a gallery has good standing, this doesn't mean that they can necessarily do well for you and your work.

This isn't to say of course that people don't have differing and varied interests, but simply that it is important to direct your attention to where you are most likely to fit naturally. And when you find your niche, nothing is more comfortable.

SOCIAL MEDIA AND THE ART WORLD

Paul Weiner

What does the art world look like today for emerging artists online? Hectic. Exciting. Disturbing.

Every day, we learn digital ways to meet new people, digest the news, buy stuff, find a lover, drool over tasty food, and even consume visual art. I set out to interview my own Instagram audience of self-selecting online art consumers in hope of finding some answers, with about 400 very opinionated respondents for each question. Their answers point to an art world that craves digital experiences and uses them to inform their real lives. Museumgoers toting selfie sticks and commercial galleries that play up their artists' Instagram fame are just the tip of the iceberg with massive, structural art world shifts looming.

THE EMERGING ART AUDIENCE IS CHANGING

Instagram is turning into a platform for visual art viewers, similar to Spotify and iTunes for music lovers. A massive online viewership uses Instagram as a search engine to seek out visual artists who satisfy their tastes - and they really care about those artists. They also recognise the absurdity of staring at art encapsulated in a tiny, low-resolution square. Polling for this piece revealed 94% of the audience wanted to see real exhibitions by the artists who they follow online, 79% see more art online than in person, and 57% think the art they find online is as important as what they see in person. With this online audience growing rapidly, massive image-quality improvements on the horizon, and a digital-native generation coming of age, a significant shift is in progress toward accepting the virtual as real.

How does this audience feel about the art world's historical power centres? 88% of the polled audience is unsatisfied with the media's contemporary art coverage and only 9% care about an artist's degree. Many respondents were discouraged by what they perceived as a top-down system that does not introduce enough new artists. On social media, by contrast, an almost unlimited number of artists are accessible at the tap of a finger. Unlike their Artforum reading forebears, the virtual public finds new artists through direct interactions without guidance from trusted art world gatekeepers. This audience looks for emerging artists who they can identify with or admire and raises them out of obscurity with little regard for prior media coverage, education, curatorial interest, or commercial success.

For the first time, artists stand to build larger audiences by connecting with the personal interests of each public viewer rather than by convincing the professional art class that they conform to elite preferences and biases. For better or worse, this means that the roles are changing for the players that have historically vetted artists before they receive public attention: curators, critics, gallerists, and the donor class. The floodgates are open – sort of.

A large audience does not predict an artist's long term importance, and it has been proven time and time again that the public's infatuations can be fleeting. The same kinds of art world players who have been in charge through much of the 20th century still control the institutional settings where art is historically canonised. The levers of power at these institutions still rely on separate audiences of their own.

Over the next few decades, it will be exciting to see if social media darling artists are able to harness public support while also convincing institutional circles that their work is imbued with an important message about the times that is worthy of being amplified and canonised. As of yet, social media success is not a fast-track to institutional acceptance in the same way a Yale MFA might be. Maybe a new generation of powerful art world figures who grow up in a digital world will embrace social media's impact.

REIMAGINING THE MUSEUM

The possibility that the museum itself will experience a virtual transformation is also worth watching.

Looking back at the 43% of those interviewed that are not convinced that art they find online is as important as art they see in real life, there is a lot of room for expansion. The polls also found that 35% were already convinced that the experience of seeing visual art online is equal to that of listening to music. The 65% who disagree might change their minds when they see the improvements coming soon to digital viewing. New extended reality (XR) headset devices satisfy cravings for greater image quality and physical experience. Take, for instance, the Magic Leap One, that, according to its creators, can "superimpose 3D computer-generated imagery over real-world objects." In combination with social media, powerful devices like these will allow us to select paintings that we find online and interact with them on the walls of the rooms we live in. Maybe our future museums will be superimposed on our own walls, where we can choose from millions of publicly available, virtually rendered artworks, and travel through history as we gaze for as long as we want, wherever we want.

SOCIAL MEDIA IS RESHAPING ARTISTS

Artists are adjusting to showing their work in digital forums, often subconsciously. These adjustments are taboo to talk about, but they are visual signifiers for the way artists share the broad struggle humans face today to exist in the digital world. The push to put out more and more attractive photos can quickly turn authenticity off in favour of the kind of calculated pop-sexiness that pulls in large audiences.

Many artists change the shapes of their works to fit in Instagram's square or edit photos of their work extensively before posting them. Other artists are addicted to the attention they can receive on social media by making very decorative paintings or finding just the right angle for a studio shot loaded with tantalising visual attractions. These concerns are a way of life that extends far outside the art world. Most of your neighbours have self-constructed identities curated for internet appearances.

At the same time, the incredible wealth of visual information available to artists who spend time on social media every day would have been unthinkable just a decade ago. Searching through popular art hashtags or following new artists brings us into new aesthetic worlds ripe for great cultural exchanges. At all hours of the day, artists from New York and Los Angeles are not only communicating with their peers in small cities in flyover states but also with artists in London, Sydney, Berlin, Dubai, or Hong Kong.

The physical object is a carrier for a digital interaction and becomes a relic of digital life. Artworks exist in a different context for each viewer and are viewed in lockstep with documentation of everyday life and constructed social personas: food photos, memes, selfies, half-naked people in swimsuits, party shots, targeted ads, and the most attractive eye candy influencers can make. As such, these works interact as much with social media's visual and algorithmic history as they do with the white-walled, white cube art history. As XR technologies become more commonplace, it will be possible to bring the work full-circle and exhibit physical paintings next to their virtual representations.

EFFECTIVE SOCIAL MEDIA – HOW TO CAPTURE YOUR AUDIENCE

In today's climate, social media is the great leveller that brings artists into contact with the people who love their work, more than ever dreamt possible. This is not to say that social media is the be-all and end-all of what it takes to be a successful artist, but what we are trying to convey is that it is an incredible tool that is immensely useful to artists, gallerists, and supporters alike.

Instagram is different things for different people, but for artists working in visual media, it is an incredibly useful business tool that can fuel your success when used effectively.

Nothing is too big to fail, and as such, it would be remiss to write an entire book about one platform whilst neglecting all others. At the time of writing, by far the most useful platform for emerging artists is Instagram, but whilst this is the case now, it would only take one or two algorithm changes to send Instagram the way of Myspace. This short essay will focus on Instagram in particular, but the approaches are translatable to those platforms we continue to see evolving today. We also aim to give you some useful techniques to bring followers from Instagram, towards more stable modes of contact such as your website and mailing list.

TYPES OF FEED

As an artist, there are two main approaches to curating your feed. Firstly, there is *The Visual Diary Approach*, which treats your feed as if it is a journal, or an online sketchbook. These feeds are often quite personal, which is useful when trying to appeal to collectors and patrons, who want to know a little more about the artist's personality before they decide to invest. This is also a good feed to utilise if you are hoping to attract galleries and curators, as these contacts want to look not only at your work, but they also like a little more information about you as a person - your interests, inspirations, methods of working, and works in progress. This kind of account is conducive to garnering a lot more genuine engagement, often promoting actual discussion within the comments. Whilst it may not generate as much overall engagement as the *Gallery Approach* outlined below, the engagement that it does generate is much more likely to create genuine connections with your fanbase, both between you and the fans, and between fans and other fans. People are much more likely to comment encouragement and critique on this type of account, and as such, it is often good to display more of your personality. You should not be afraid of sharing your insecurities and failures as well as your triumphs, as all of this humanises you and helps your supporters feel like they know the real you. This makes fans and collectors invest in the artist, rather than just the artwork. With this approach, your captions and responses to comments or messages can be a lot more informal and conversational than you might think, which is great because as well as being nicer to write, they are also nicer to read.

Secondly, there is the *Gallery Approach*, which is the kind of account that shows very little personality in favour of expertly taken images of works on pristine white gallery-like walls. The captions are often formal and written in the third person, with the artist's voice largely absent.

This account is successful is when the artist is already established and doesn't need or want this direct connection with their supporters. It is also good for practitioners like commercial illustrators and designers, as learning more about the personality of the artist is less important for commissioning editors or art directors than it is for collectors.

Both types of account can be useful for different reasons, so you should spend some time deciding which suits you and what you want, to achieve the best results.

DRIVING ENGAGEMENT

There are many ways to drive engagement on your social media, but most of all it is important that this engagement is genuine.

What you want is comments, reposts, direct messages, and likes - ideally in that order. When it comes to comments, you want ones that go beyond the ubiquitous 'great work', and give something more human. There are many accounts that, in order to drive engagement on their own account, will copy and paste the same banal-but-generally-complimentary text into the comments of every photo they scroll past, and it is not these kinds of comments that we are seeking.

Whilst it is true that indeed *any* comments will help drive overall engagement, what is more useful is the actual conversation that is so possible within comments.

Wherever possible, we would recommend liking the comments your photos receive, and even better, responding to them. It has taken the commenter valuable time to click into the dialogue box and type something out, and when the collective attention-span is as short as it now is (especially on Instagram), this is significant. It is nice for the commenter to see that their act has not gone unnoticed, and it also helps drive engagement to their account too. Social media is social in more than just name, and so the more you engage with people (on both their accounts and your own), the more they will engage with you in turn.

As well as encouraging engagement on your own account, you should be giving what you hope to receive across other people's accounts too.

You should comment upon works you love and say why you love them; don't stick to the ubiquitous single word affirmatives or banal thumbs-up emojis. Don't offer critique unless it is requested though, as it is hard to judge tone without body-language, and you don't want to appear to be derisory.

Some of the most successful accounts that we know of post their own work as often as sharing the work of others, and whilst this may seem counterintuitive, it pays dividends. Accounts that share other's work are by their very nature more-varied, and so necessarily, they are more widely-appealing. It is important to share images that won't look out of place amongst your works, as a well-curated feed is a must. When done well, these additions can benefit the whole, which becomes greater than the sum of its parts. This can be done in either posts or stories, and both are good for different reasons. Stories are temporary and immediate, and are somewhat-free of the negative effects of the selective algorithm that govern what is seen when. When sharing a work to a story, tag the artist always, as unless you do this, they won't know you've posted. By promoting dialogue between you and the artists, it creates the potential for them to further share your profile through reposts.

CAPTURING YOUR AUDIENCE

So as particular social media platforms are always at risk of fading into obscurity, what can you do with this audience once you have them?

What you need is to bring them from your social media to something a little closer to home – there are a few ways to do this. Ideally, you want them to visit your shows and buy your work, but both of these things happen in the real, physical world, and there often needs to be one or two more steps in between this and them discovering you online.

One such step is your website, or more specifically, a blog. As outlined above, your website is now not your most efficient tool when it comes to making your work discoverable by potentially interested-parties, but it is still an incredibly useful tool in bringing them in a little closer, and giving them more information about yourself and your practice.

A website serves many functions that are absent from your social media, making a well-ordered website essential. The most efficient website would contain a blog, which when used effectively can help drive traffic *towards* social media and vice-versa. Keywords and an effective SEO (Search Engine Optimisation) approach are useful to optimise how the blog performs online (SEO is actually a lot easier than it sounds).

The ideal blog would be updated as often as is possible, and contain more text than images. This can be used to provide further insight into your practice or your inspirations.

The optimum use of a website/blog can work wonders not only for your online presence (in terms of SEO and being 'searchable'), but it can also supplement your social media. The content that you present should be specific to each medium (main website, blog, and social media), as each of them has different strengths and weaknesses. For the main website, this should contain all details such as personal statement and CV, as well as a list of other engagements such as shows you've been in and other relevant information. The images here should be the high-resolution photos of finished works, shown either cropped to only include the work, or in an interesting setting. Think of this as a retrospective show, and only include your absolute best work. The blog can be a bit more informal, contain a lot more text, and talk about things as they are in progress. This can link to your social media, and where appropriate build upon or give more detail to things you have posted there. Social media should be used as outlined above, but all three should be used so as to direct traffic to the other two, either by using direct links, or by explaining where this extra content can be found.

Another place that you want to be bringing your social media following is into your mailing list. Whilst we can say with certainty that social media as a concept will be around forever, we cannot say the same with any degree of certainty for individual platforms. As suggested earlier, each platform, however stable it may seem now, is in a tenuous place. It would only take a few minor changes to the way any platform works to destroy it irrevocably, or for another slightly more workable one to emerge, and all of your hard-won followers are lost.

One thing that will be around forever however, is email. When done correctly, a solid mailing list can be the lifeblood of your business. Something you should start doing immediately if you aren't already, is encouraging your followers to transition to also being on your mailing list. Whenever anyone buys or expresses interest in your work, put all of their details in a spreadsheet to keep a record. This gives you a bank of people who you can be certain have a tangible interest in your work. Whenever you release a new print or start planning a new show, these are the most likely people to be interested. Once you start doing this, you will wish you did it sooner.

Some ways that are possible to get people to sign up to your mailing list include using swipe-up functionality within stories (if available), adding your signup address in your bio, or mentioning your mailing list in your captions. The mailing list signup box can appear as a pop-up on your website, or remain permanently in a side-bar, but whatever way you encourage sign-ups, make sure you are GDPR compliant. Whilst it *is* still permissible to copy-and-paste email addresses into your mailing list yourself, be wary that it must be of genuine interest to these people, and that they have in some way consented to be contacted by you. If you ignore these rules, you run the risk of being blacklisted. When people unsubscribe from a mailing list they have the option to explain their reasons for doing so, with one of the tick-boxes being 'I never signed up for this list'. The more of these you get, the more likely your provider is to ban you.

Unsubscribes happen to everyone, and should not be seen as fans that have changed their minds about you or your work; people unsubscribe for a multitude of reasons. Think of it as part of a honing of a tight, dedicated list that has a genuine interest in what you are doing. Don't despair.

You can optimise the open rates of your mailing lists using techniques such as personalising the 'To' field of your message, verifying your email and authenticating your domain. These adjustments are a little fiddly, but they will really help ensure your messages do not get redirected to junk by spam filters.

To conclude, your social media should be treated as a business tool, and when used appropriately can be of great benefit to you. It is something that is often seen as adolescent and throwaway, and many artists neglect to treat it with the respect it deserves. It is true that the platforms that are popular currently may not be around forever, but what is inarguable is that social media in some form or other, will be. What is important is to not fear change, and utilise whatever new media is available in the most efficient way possible. If that means getting the best out of Instagram now whilst it is around and then adopting something else that may come along to replace it, then do so.

To use this media in the most efficient way is to bring any followers you attain closer into the fold, to create a like-minded community. Once you have this community, you should strive to extend that community *beyond* the confines of whatever platform you found them on, and towards other more stable platforms like email.

HOW DO YOU SELECT ARTISTS FOR EXHIBITIONS?

NO GALLERY

I look to be taught new ways to think about ideas, medium and process

MAUREEN PALEY

Carefully

KRUPIC KERSTING

A. By recommendation from artists and curators
B. Seeing shows and visiting art school presentations
C. Social media

PUBLIC GALLERY

Fundamentally we have to love the work, and see it fitting in with our programme

CHARLIE MILLS OF COLLECTIVE ENDING, BOLD TENDENCIES, AND HANNAH BARRY GALLERY

It depends on the scale and nature of the show, there's a lot of pressure on people to work with new artists and stay ahead of the game. Often it's far more productive to work with the same artists over time, much like a gallery does, building your relationship with them. In other cases, it's a once in a lifetime opportunity and you just gotta go for it

KRISTIN HJELLEGJERDE GALLERY

From the first instinctual heartbeat when I see a work that makes me feel I have not seen this before

THE ROLE OF THE GALLERY IN THE POST-SOCIAL-MEDIA WORLD

WHAT ARE GALLERIES FOR?

This question would have been much easier to answer twenty years ago, before the dawn of social media and the online exhibition space. It is also a question we asked ourselves in 2017 when we launched Delphian.

Social media has given us all an infinite connect-ability, spanning oceans and time-zones at almost light-speed. It is easier than ever to see and be seen, and now collectors and fans can find artists, visit their studios, and get to know them personally without ever having to leave their own homes. Social media creates opportunities that simply didn't exist before, but they also prove a vehicle for greater competition.

Artists are now freer than ever to connect with and sell to fans and collectors from their own studios, and collectors are becoming less gallery-loyal. The former middlemen of the art industry are increasingly removed from the processes of discovery and purchase.

It is now not just a select few behemoth galleries that hold all of the power in determining which artists will succeed and which will falter, as collectors no-longer require the validation of these institutions before deciding who and what they will support. Art-fans and collectors can now discover artists who may have never exhibited before and can acquire their work long before its price has inflated beyond affordability. The role of galleries is not the discoverer-patron-gatekeeper that it once was, and for emerging and mid-level galleries to survive, they need to adapt to this new pattern or suffer for it. The art world is changing, and this can be destructive if responded to as a threat rather than a challenge to be overcome. Galleries that fear this evolution risk becoming isolated and defensive, which will only serve to harm their interests in the long run.

This is not a scathing critique of traditional galleries, nor a statement of authority, but rather an impassioned and subjective call-to-arms.

We as gallerists should see this democratisation of the art world as a freeing and exciting revitalisation that we welcome with fresh ideas.

WHAT ARE THESE FRESH APPROACHES THAT GALLERIES CAN NOW TAKE?

Galleries, on the whole, are able to take a much more collaborative approach to how they do business in this information-rich, infinitely-sharable new world that we find ourselves in. Galleries have the ability to become 'connectors' in the truest sense of the word, and what that has meant in the past is not what it means now. Before social media and the internet, galleries were first-and-foremost where people discovered and viewed art. Now, for better or worse, this is not the case. People find and view a huge proportion of the art that they encounter on a screen, and this creates a void around what the traditional gallery once was.

Galleries are now not the only ones who possess the insider knowledge of what is and isn't worthwhile. People don't need the validation of what is good or investment-savvy, as all of this validation can now come by democratic, online channels. That is not to say that what is successful on social media will be successful in the real world, but that there are many freely-accessible metrics with which anyone can make an informed decision as to what they think is worth their time, investment, or interest. Galleries need to step back from this role, and rather than attempting to retain their grasp on this, they should attempt to become the conduit through which people discover great artwork, wherever it is located.

This may seem counterintuitive to what is essentially a business based upon the selling of artworks, as to do this well, galleries must be sharing great works that are located all over the art world in a way that will directly benefit (what was once called) their competitors. To attempt to survive as a gallery, only sharing your list of perhaps 13 represented artists (and a similar amount that you show in group shows) day-in-day-out, is a surefire way to curate a very repetitive feed that may lose followers, and visibility, in the long-term. In the days of old, showing the same 13 artists was fine, as perhaps less than half of them will do solo shows with you once a year, and the rest will alternate to the following year. Now, there is pressure on galleries to be posting new works so as to not sink to the bottom of the pile, and this does not allow for the traditional only-represented-artists model. This isn't to say that galleries shouldn't still represent artists in the same way (in fact it's imperative that they do), but rather they need to be sharing their platform with artists whom they don't directly work with.

Galleries are not like hairdressers, to whom we forge lasting bonds. We do not find one gallery we like and only ever view the work they show. Instead, we visit many, and like what we like from many all at once.

ENGAGING WITH GALLERIES

To an outsider, the art world can seem impenetrable. The most common concern for an emerging artist is how to get their work seen, and then exhibited, by galleries.

Some galleries will accept submissions via email, but most won't. If you do decide to go down this route, first make sure that the galleries you intend to contact do indeed accept submissions this way, and second, make sure that they are the right fit for your work.

It is pointless sending unsolicited emails to a gallery that doesn't accept submissions this way, as they will invariably be deleted, most often without being opened and the contents seen. Furthermore, an email with multiple attachments is going to take up valuable storage space in a gallery's inbox, and so will have to be deleted if it is not essential to what it is they are doing - this has to be done individually and by hand. Although your work may not be seen, it is possible that your name will be remembered subconsciously in a negative light.

If a gallery does accept email submissions, you need to make sure that your work would fit nicely in with what they are doing. There is no use emailing a gallery who deals in 18th century woodcuts and asking them to consider your VR video piece. It's infinitely better to know your audience, and not to waste the time of a gallery that is never going to be the right fit for what you're doing in the first place.

Once you have made sure the gallery does accept submissions, and that they would be the right fit for your work, it is important that you closely follow their submission guidelines. Submission guidelines are very carefully written and are there to make both yours and the gallery's lives easier. Blanket emailing lots of galleries in the hope that the ones that will suit your work will be the ones that respond is unlikely to yield good results. It is easy to spot a copy-and-paste message that has been sent to multiple recipients and this practice can make you look unprofessional.

The art world is based upon human relationships much more than it may at first appear, and as such you should treat gallerists and curators as people. The art world is a community, and as with any community, you need to contribute to it rather than just attempting to take from it. Go to private views and rave about the good ones you see. Find a gallery that you love, and tell the world.

Comment regularly on their posts with genuine responses to what they are doing. Support them in any way you can. Start a blog, write about art, share your excitement for the world you hope to spend your career.

As outlined by Hector Campbell later in this book, you don't even have to wait for someone to come along and hand you a show; you can go out and make your own in whatever space you can find. These DIY types of shows are often the most exciting to visit, and although they might not look the most professional, they are the ones that have a lasting impact. Curators and gallerists visit these, and the ones that make an impression are not soon forgotten.

Showing initiative is a great way to get your work out there, as well as showing people that you are willing to work hard, and think creatively. A good business-ethic goes a long way, and artists who are self-initiating projects without the support of an established gallery are displaying their seriousness to all that are watching, and even if it is difficult to quantify, the right people *are* watching.

Gallerists and curators entire careers are focused on discovering amazing art, and showing it to the world.

Accordingly, they often don't like to be told where this exciting work can be found. Instead of contacting a gallery or curator and trying to convince them of how great you and your work is, it is often better to make yourself discoverable and entice the gallerists and curators to come to you. The most effective way to do this is to engage with them genuinely and to support others in ways you wish to be supported. These things happen reciprocally, so if you are engaging with the art world in a genuine way, others will start to engage with you also.

The more active you are in a certain section of the art world, the more visible you will be. If you have greater visibility, so too will your work. This is by far the most successful and pleasant way to engage with galleries.

GETTING PEOPLE THROUGH THE DOOR

Media coverage can play a crucial role in the development of an artist's career, both in the visibility of their practice and the final stage of the creative process – the exhibition. Exhibitions are made to be seen, which is why promotion plays such a vital part in attracting an audience.

A private view may generate new interest and lead to sales, but how do you get people to attend your exhibition in the first place?

Primarily, it is important to think carefully about how you promote your show. Even if you think you have perfected every detail of the show itself, without effective promotion it can be difficult for your exhibition to gain the attention it deserves.

Galleries will promote their exhibitions through their own channels, but this should not stop the artist from learning how to do it themselves to their own networks. The first time an artist sets about promoting an exhibition can be intimidating, but it is a perfect opportunity to start learning marketing skills which will help other aspects of their artistic practice.

When promoting an exhibition there are many avenues to pursue, from social media, blogs, magazines (both online and printed), and many more. We will cover these tools separately but before we start we must point out that inevitably media outlets, writers, and publishers receive far more submissions than they can ever write about. Artists should learn to grow a thick skin when it comes to emails and submissions being rejected, or more often ignored. Artists should always make sure to research extensively first before contacting the person/organisation to make sure that the exhibition fits their editorial style and the type of work they publicise. A targeted approach is always recommended and inevitably more successful.

Before contacting anyone you should make sure to have the core materials for your exhibition completed and ready to send out. These are the invitation, the press release, and some images of artworks in the exhibition.

For the invitation, make sure to include all the details that people need to know - dates, times, addresses and contact information. This should be bold and striking so that the highest number of people take notice. Several versions of the invitation should be made to fit all the various dimensions specified by social media platforms.

Press releases, aside from the core details outlined above, should also include the full "what, when, how, and why" - with the "why" being extremely important as any publisher will want to know what makes your exhibition newsworthy. A good rule to follow is to produce an insightful and informative description of the work, themes behind it, and information about the artist themselves. All of this should be written in the third person as this makes it as easy as possible for the publisher to rewrite it for their own output - or even just copy and paste it. The text should be accessible, so avoid too much art-world jargon. Describing the work in the exhibition in a good amount of detail, with sections that can be lifted and tweaked, will enable the potential reviewer to produce a piece for a listings site without having seen the exhibition. A quote from the artist relating to the work is also a useful item to include as this gives an extra level of depth to the story.

Good-quality images of the artworks in the exhibition are essential, as it is counterproductive to put in all that time and effort producing a strong body of work only for it to be ignored by publishers due to poor-quality reproductions. Photographs of the pieces should be clear, well-lit, high-resolution, and should show the work in the best way possible for people who can't see it in the flesh. Don't fall at the last hurdle.

Images should be sized to around 1200px on the longest side and saved as RGB format for maximum compatibility on online platforms, but publishers may contact you with their own image size requirements.

BLOGS AND MAGAZINES

Sending details of the exhibition to relevant blogs and magazines should be the main weapon in your marketing armoury, as these outlets will be the best chance to get the word out about the exhibition to a new and larger audience. Make sure you send them the details (press release, low-resolution images which are sized for web, links to the event pages and online details) in good time so that they have a chance to post it within their deadlines. For printed magazines, press releases should be sent out at least three months ahead of the exhibition date. Magazine lead-times are long and they will need time to write the articles before their print dates. For online, at least a month before is usually good. After this, follow up with another email or phone call to chase them after a reasonable amount of time has passed. If there has been no response after two attempts at contact, this should be taken as a rejection on that occasion, but don't lose heart - you will get a lot of these.

With regards to online and printed media coverage, there are generally two avenues of contact; freelance writers, and the blogs and magazines themselves. It may seem on the surface that freelance writers are a better bet as they have the freedom to try and sell articles to a variety of publications but there is no guarantee (unless agreed beforehand) that anything they offer will be published.

Blogs and magazines will usually have submission guidelines on their website and these should be followed to the letter. Avoid the temptation to "stand out from the crowd" by doing something out of the ordinary. If the submission doesn't adhere to the guidelines, nine times out of ten it will be instantly ignored.

LISTINGS SITES

The importance of listings sites is often overlooked but these can be an invaluable way of expanding an audience easily, as you are tapping into the audience that regularly check these sites. Many listings sites will send out regular emails to their subscribers with all the latest exhibition openings, artist opportunities, and more. Being included in these is simple, and instantly boosts the profile of the exhibition. Research online for as many as you can find and fill in their submission forms.

PRINTED MARKETING MATERIALS

A much less-used medium for exhibition promotion these days is printed materials, and it shouldn't be as this can make you stand out from the crowd. In this digital era, everything revolves around PDFs and social media feeds - but magazines and press outlets still have postal addresses, and these are a direct route for getting a press release in front of publishers. Imagine their surprise as a beautifully presented envelope arrives for a journalist with a bold, arresting invitation inside. They will be receiving tens if not hundreds of submissions per day in their inbox, but nowhere near (if any) that many in their physical mailbox, and so flyers, printed press releases, and other personalised touches are a sure-fire way to stand apart from the background noise of other submissions. If you do this, it is a good idea to also submit via the usual channels too.

SOCIAL MEDIA

Posting about the exhibition across all your social media platforms a good amount of time before the opening is essential to build excitement.

Creating a central Facebook event that all social media promotion can link back to is a very easy way to reach a large number of people for free. If there is some advertising budget, Facebook ads or boosted page posts to promote the event further work well. There are many good resources online to help guide you through using Facebook advertising.

On Instagram, make sure you search for relevant hashtags that relate to the exhibition that you are showing and add them to your posts. Include a mixture of hashtags with a large number of posts and smaller ones too to get the largest spread of people engaging with you. Think about also creating a unique hashtag that relates to the exhibition - either the title of the show or a related theme. Encourage people who view the exhibition to tag any posts with the hashtag and this can serve as an archive, and a place to send people afterwards where they can see everyone's coverage of the exhibition. Another important thing to remember to do is to change your Instagram bio link to the Facebook event so that people can sign up, growing the numbers and increasing the visibility of the event across people's feeds.

When combined, all these separate tools create an incredibly powerful approach to engaging with media outlets over the range of platforms.

OTHER SKILLS
An Interview with Jordy Kerwick

D How did you get started?

JK By getting obsessed with making work, and learning by extreme failure. It's a compulsive passion where there is no endgame.

D You're very vocal in your support of other artists, and you aren't competitive in the same way that some artists are.

JK I get more enjoyment out of giving presents than receiving – if everyone's doing well, that speaks volumes for the industry. People helped me, and so I think why shouldn't I pay it forward? I think it's the right thing to do, and I'm eternally grateful for the people that have helped me. I think it's important to create a community instead of slogging away by yourself because it's lonely that way. You're constantly reviewing your performance and questioning yourself, and it's a real deep slide to the bottom – if you make it 'me versus the world'.

D What would be one piece of advice that you would give to early-career artists just starting out?

JK Henry Miller once said that you have to be "obsessed and possessed" and I think that this is the greatest advice you could ever give. That doesn't apply to just art, but to any vocation. It means draw as much as you can, read as much as you can, and just give it your all. I think that a lot of people take a really tepid approach, and I get it, it's fear of failure. There are a lot of reasons not to throw your all into something, but I think the commitment is important.

D You have a background in marketing and branding, how much of your success can you attribute to that knowledge-set?

JK I think a fair bit. In my previous life, I was far from successful, but I learned a lot. People's perception of you is their reality, so you have to have that in mind. I think it's really important to be wary of your 'brand' – authenticity is the key.

D If you could – what is something that you would change about the art world?

JK I have been really lucky in the people that I've worked with, but I guess if anything, the art institutions have created a pathway for artists that's just not realistic. Not having any formal marketing, branding, business-development education puts artists (from day one post-university) in a very precarious position. I'm not anti-establishment at all, but if you take the fact that you need to promote yourself as a business so as to be able to make more work, or pay rent, you need to know how to market yourself. You need to know how to have conversations, you need to know how to manage a brand (the brand being you), and I don't think that's taught enough. There needs to be more conversations around how to manage yourself as a business.

D Too few working artists think of themselves as businesses.

JK I think when you take away the glamour, it's really unromantic to even talk about it. Art is supposed to be a realm of make-believe and endless possibilities, which is beautiful, but someone has got to pay the bills and buy more canvas. Unless you're an outlier and are able to secure relationships with the top-end galleries at the ripe old age of 21, for the 99.9% of us its...

D Spreadsheets.

JK Yeah, you've got to be on your toes. You've got to be having uncomfortable conversations about prices and sales for example. Social media is good as you are able to network and have discussions with people. My value does not come in big groups, I really struggle. For me, meeting people at openings would actually be counterproductive, so having the capacity to have nice conversations with people all around the world online is really good.

So that's the thing I'd change: getting people more training, more understanding around marketing, networking, and how to have these discussions with people. Making sure you portray yourself as a good person: no-one wants to work with difficult people with false sense of self, people want to work with cool people who appreciate opportunities.

REQUIEM FOR THE EXHIBITION – HOW ALL ARTISTS MUST BECOME CURATORS

The exhibition is, and forever should be thought of by artists, curators, and the viewer as one coherent artwork, which should be encountered accordingly. An artist who defers complete curatorial power over to an external player, abandons their responsibility to ensure that their work be encountered in the correct way, so as to afford the viewer the best tools with which to approach the work.

Viewers, upon encountering an artwork, have an entire and unquantifiable cache of past lived experience that influences their deciphering of stimuli. This means that as artists we have very little power over each individual reading of our work. Although this is not a problem in itself, it means that we must do all that we can to carefully place our work within a setting in which it is most naturally at ease.

Each work of art is different, and as such, every piece will have its own optimum setting in which to be seen. A painting seen under a cold white gallery light will appear completely different when seen illuminated by the sun via a skylight in the artist's studio.

The currently commonly adopted approach of hanging similarly-sized works at eye-level or all in relation to one central line that runs around the gallery, allows the viewer to stand motionless in the middle of the space, simply rotating their head until they feel like they have seen all of the works. This is of course something that happens not by choice on the part of the viewer, rather subconsciously. It can discourage people to get up close to the works, and thus does a disservice to the individual pieces, as well as to the exhibition on the whole. Idiosyncrasies can be lost in this scenario, as the viewer is not encouraged to really interact with the works.

Whilst this may indeed be the optimum way in which to evaluate some works, it can't help but be far from being so for *all* works.

Artists must consider, and respond to the space in which their work will be encountered, and then engage with it in a way that benefits both the work and the space itself. An exhibition should add something ephemeral to the works, in a way that captures people's attention and sparks a dialogue between the individual works – otherwise, why group them together at all – and with the space they are within.

It is possible that in curating one cohesive show, that something from each work is lost in favour of the whole. It is similar to how some of the finesse with which a trapeze artist flies through the air may be lost when there are also lion-tamers and fire-breathers all vying for your attention at the circus. This is most certainly negligible, as what is lost from the individual is gained by the whole, and despite one risking missing out on some of the minutiae within single works when viewed in this way, the whole is greater than the sum of its constituent parts. The circus is more exciting than a lone trapeze artist precisely because of all the bravado, distraction, and theatre.

The exhibition creates a unified whole that feeds off its component parts, and is captivating in its temporality. The effect is of one immersive artwork comprised of many smaller artworks symbiotically supporting the coherent whole. And once the show is over, the works are then renewed with whatever details they may have temporarily lent to the show, and they are enlivened, seeming even more special than they were before.

It would not be suggested that an artist allow into their studio someone whom they do not yet know, and give them some control over how each artwork looks. Yet when approaching an exhibition this is the norm, for a curator often decides how and where the works are hung.

As curators ourselves we know of a very real need both to curate and be curated - however we believe that artists should take heed of how their work will be seen in a gallery setting, and not miss the very special opportunity to create (or help create) what can be a magical experience for all parties. Curation occupies a legitimate and necessary place in the art world, and long may it continue to do so. The gallery is a canvas, and it is one that is often left un-painted: an unaware act of self censorship.

The act of displaying artworks requires a huge amount of thought and attention, so as to allow them to be contemplated considerately. For this reason, defined roles are important. A curator's job is to curate, but the artist should have some input into this process whenever possible. Artists should view the exhibition as a joint responsibility, and not take this salient undertaking lightly.

An exhibition is a collaboration between artist and gallery/curator, and should be viewed as such by all involved. Not only because it is imperative that the work is seen in its best light possible, but also so as to not allow the physical exhibition to become less and less relevant to the art-viewing public.

These days, due to the dawn of social media and the internet, the way in which we encounter artwork has changed. The vast majority of the art we view is on a screen. A backlit image, presented within a format the size of either a phone or laptop screen, inherently limits what we can and cannot discern. Due to this, the brighter, less detailed paintings are rising to the top, as they are the ones that suit the inflexible format best. Whilst social media and the internet are great tools to be ignored by artists at their peril, we must strive to bring the exhibition up to date with the rest of the formats in which art is encountered. This is not to say that how we use social media must change, but simply that we need to acknowledge that the ways in which we view the *majority* of the art we see is now not as it once was – in person, but rather, on a digital platform.

This paradigm-shift in presentation also puts at risk the more traditional gallery in general, as artists and their interested public can now engage on a one-to-one basis, rather than necessitating the middleman of the commercial gallery. Artists are now more able than ever to populate an open studio with collectors than they ever have been, and sell to them directly if the chance arises.

I'm sure that whilst we all agree that work must be seen in the flesh to fully appreciate it, we must also not blind ourselves to the fact that people now view only a small proportion of art in this way. People are much more willing to buy art unseen now, as they can see a fairly good facsimile online.

Online exhibitions can be a great thing when done correctly, and they offer possibilities to artists and curators that simply wouldn't exist otherwise, but their existence naturally necessitates this re-contemplation of what a traditional, physical exhibition is. This need not be a cause for concern nor a rejection of the past, but rather it should allow us to rethink and adapt how we intend to present these physical works when we do.

WHAT IS THE ONE THING ABOUT THE ART WORLD THAT YOU WISH WOULD DISAPPEAR FOREVER?

RICHIE CULVER
Some of my early works

DAISY PARRIS
The exploitation of young artists

JAKE CHAPMAN
Paint

TOM ANHOLT
The obsession with finding trends

ROWAN NEWTON
Galleries playing it safe

HEDLEY ROBERTS
Wannabe artists, curators, gallerists and dealers. These are really tough jobs to do well, they're not lifestyle options

NEVA HOSKING
Networking!

FLORENCE HUTCHINGS
Art school snobbishness

CATHERINE HAGGARTY
Sometimes – Instagram. But mostly white men who control shows and advertising and sales. Diversity is needed!

HAYDEN KAYS
The thinking that it is of more importance than the real world

MAKING YOUR OWN OPPORTUNITIES – THE BENEFITS OF DIY EXHIBITIONS AND NON TRADITIONAL SPACES

Hector Campbell

For an emerging artist keen to exhibit, almost anywhere could be seen as an opportunity: storage units, car parks, shop fronts, telephone boxes, shopping centres, churches, crypts, living rooms, pub cellars, billboards, lamp posts, or fences. In fact, the above are all places that have been co-opted intermittently to host exhibitions, as an increasing number of emerging artists and curators eschew the traditional, inaccessible 'white cube' gallery model. The reasons for this adoption of non-traditional exhibition spaces as a modus operandi are numerous, as are the unique pros and cons. With a myriad of motivations, advantages, and disadvantages for doing so, a number can be illustrated by looking at three particular artist-led case studies: The Parasite, The Shopping Centre, and The Pub.

THE PARASITE

"The Parasite started as a way for us to exhibit work at a time when it felt so important to do so. Despite being a wall-based cabinet, we still treated it like a proper space." Victor Seaward, artist, and curator

The Parasite is a vitrine designed and fabricated by artist Victor Seaward, that was attached to the side of the Royal College of Art's Sackler Building, acting as both a project space and an extension of Seaward's own artistic practice. Intended as a nomadic micro-gallery, it is aptly named by nature of it's benefitting from the pre-existing visibility and footfall of its host building, despite no financial commitment from them. It has been used to host exhibitions curated by both Seaward himself, as well as invited friends, artists, and curators. Described by Seaward as an 'industrial, post-luxury display vitrine', The Parasite was conceived during the then postgraduate student's desire to flex his curatorial muscles whilst continuing his own artistic exploration of display, presentation, and containment. It also functioned as a productive alternative to having to rent his own project space. The Parasite, therefore, exemplifies a couple of the key benefits of utilising a non-traditional gallery space.

Firstly, the ability to operate against financial constraints and the accepted conventions of renting that control the project space system. Secondly, the increased visibility garnered for an exhibition by existing within pre-established areas of public foot-traffic. The financial overheads of The Parasite are almost negligible, for, after the initial costs of construction and installation, it can subsist with minimal interruption. There is no need for gallery invigilation (a task that, especially at an emerging art level, frequently falls on the curator or artists involved) and no rent to pay thanks to its inherent, conceptual, parasitic nature. On the other hand, the exhibitions it houses receive an increased level of exposure, in part due to their instantaneous 24-hour access (no need for opening hours and/or appointments), and their egalitarian, welcoming accessibility (uncommon amongst especially the larger commercial galleries).

A bonus benefit of The Parasite, and a commonality of many of the non-traditional spaces, is the exciting site-specificity that occurs as a consequence of the physical restraints the 'absurdly small space' of the vitrine puts upon exhibiting artists. The invited artists are forced to directly respond to the confines of the space, resulting in artworks and exhibitions that could only take place within The Parasite, as well as an engaging ephemerality that is frequently lost within the neutral, neutered 'white cube' gallery system.

Two of those invited to stage an exhibition within The Parasite were artists and curators Billy Fraser & Nelle Gevers, whose threefold exhibition project 'Extended Call' echoes one of the most notable examples of both the use of a non-traditional space and of an artist-led exhibition – 1988's three-part exhibition 'Freeze', staged by then-Goldsmiths student Damien Hirst.

Fraser and Gever's 'Extended Call' series – which aimed to critique both the idea of public display and the accessibility, or lack thereof, of contemporary art – began by colonising ten red telephone boxes around Soho, Central London (free, available public spaces – a prime target for artistic adoption), and replacing any pre-existing erotic calling cards with a range of artist-designed postcards. Part two was hosted at The Parasite and saw the same artists creating miniature works in response to the physical challenges presented by the space, especially in the context of The Parasite's first group exhibition. The third and final installment of 'Extended Call' was held at Subsidiary Projects, which falls into the popular, ever-increasing bracket of living-room exhibition spaces, by existing within the front room of a Vauxhall domicile.

The Parasite, and projects such as 'Extended Call', embody the possibilities and advantages available to artists who think outside of the 'white cube' and demonstrate how this artist-led, DIY ethos of many non-traditional spaces and the exhibitions they host result in unique, site-specific artworks and shows that benefit from the accessibility, visibility, and freedom that such spaces provide.

"Rough, ready and playful freedom can get lost in so-called traditional 'white-walled' gallery spaces. I was interested to incorporate and respond to the building's architecture, something afforded by curating in a non-traditional space." Cara Mills, artist, and curator

Towards the tail end of 2018, Whiteleys shopping centre in Queensway welcomed a group of young artists to undertake a residency programme within the third floor of the Grade II Listed building, which also hosted the resulting exhibition 'Inhabiting The Dome', curated by artist Cara Mills. Unlike The Parasite, and due to Whiteleys being officially closed for redevelopment, 'Inhabiting The Dome' could not benefit from the pre-existing visitor numbers of the once-popular department store, nor could it boast easy accessibility, with appointments required for viewing after the opening night and quite the list of instructions and signs to follow in order to find it. However, these drawbacks inherent of some residential, or industrial, non-traditional spaces were outweighed by the special, unrepeatable artistic responses to Whiteleys' celebrated architecture and significant history that emerged during the project.

Using large-scale and performative artworks to activate the now uninhabited space (alongside displays of more conventional paintings and sculpture) the building itself became an active participant and contributor to 'Inhabiting the Dome'. As part of the exhibition's opening night the titular Whiteleys dome (which equals the size of your average planetarium), was animated with the use of light projections designed by multimedia artists such as Mowgli (Manuel Barrio) and Alice Kilkenny - created in direct response to its position as a recognisable and historic central landmark. Indeed many of the invited artists leapt at the chance to exhibit works that either directly or indirectly referenced their renowned and unique surroundings.

Exhibitions such as 'Inhabiting the Dome', and similar artist-initiated residency programmes, that occupy residential or industrial spaces may sacrifice some of the easy accessibility and visibility afforded to more traditional gallery spaces and exhibitions, however, those artists who choose to stray off the beaten track and embrace them are rewarded with the opportunity to create works imbued with inimitable site-specificity and exclusive ephemerality.

THE PUB

"Absinthe under one name brings together a variety of different people and talents, all working towards a shared concept and collectivism within Central London. The project has become a perfect testing-ground for a less-traditional approach to making and showing art today." Billy Fraser, artist and curator

Expanding on some of the concepts initiated with his aforementioned 'Extended Call' project, Billy Fraser teamed up with Charlie Mills (artist liaison of Peckham's brilliant Hannah Barry Gallery), and James Capper (prominent mechanical sculptor), to create 'Absinthe' – a public programme of exhibitions, installations, performances, and events in The Spit and Sawdust pub in South London. Acting under the moniker Collective Ending, the three curators entered into a mutually-beneficial partnership with the pub, to launch a series of three-month-long exhibitions, each featuring twenty seven artists representing the stranger side of London's emerging art scene.

'Absinthe' could be seen as Fraser's perfection of the artist-led, non-traditional exhibition model, marrying many of the advantages we have observed with The Parasite – notably extended, egalitarian accessibility (the exhibitions can be viewed whenever the pub is open), parasitic expropriation of the existing audience, and both financial and creative freedom (The Spit and Sawdust and Collective Ending exist in a not-for-profit partnership, with the former respecting the artistic requirements and desires of the latter, within reason) – with those realized by Cara Mills and 'Inhabiting the Dome' at Whiteleys. These include site-specific responses to the space (many of the Absinthe artists directly incorporate aspects of the pub's history, function, and furnishings within their works) and an activation or revitalisation of a once vibrant social site (the pub has benefitted from the patronage of Absinthe's extended artistic community). This unique combination of advantages, as well as Collective Ending's resultant creative independence and art-world emancipation, has seen the 'Absinthe' exhibitions become a strange staple in the London cultural calendar, attracting esteemed exhibiting artists allowing for the presentation of some innovative artist-run events.

Exhibitions such as 'Inhabiting The Dome', projects such as 'Absinthe' and 'Extended Call', and the endeavours of artists such as Victor Seaward, Billy Fraser, and Cara Mills, make a strong case for the idea that utilising non-traditional gallery spaces is not only a cost-effective way for emerging artists to stage exhibitions of their work (and that of their contemporaries), but also a viable, and in some instances superior alternative to operating within the conventional confines of the art world gallery system. The artistic autonomy awarded to those artists that find enterprising and innovative methods of exhibiting not only allows for the enactment of their singular, pure artistic intention but also consequentially leads to an increased awareness of their work and a memorable, momentary experience for the audience.

THE PITFALLS OF SELLING

This is often considered to be the dirty side of the art world; a side that it seems indiscreet to discuss, but it is one that is necessary if artists are to survive as creatives. Artists need to sell works so as to facilitate the creation of more works, and the more they sell, the more freedom they have to spend their time creating unencumbered.

So how do artists make sellable work, and then how do you sell it? While this is not a magic checklist for upping the "value" of your work, here are a few points about how to avoid falling into some very common traps that can hinder your success.

1. DON'T OVERPRODUCE

This can be a tricky one to conform to, as artists are often so excited by their process that they make, and subsequently share, as much as possible. This is damaging in a few ways:

Firstly, not everything that you make will be amazing - this is a fact. Not even everything Van Gogh made was amazing. It is important (and entirely necessary) to experiment and be prolific, but it is perhaps more important to not allow any old thing out of your studio. Most of these experiments are just that, experiments, that aren't fully-resolved works of art.

Once something is let out of your studio it becomes an autonomous object that will likely outlive even you, so only let out your absolute best work. This isn't to say that you should make less, only that you should release or show less.

Another negative of overproduction is the reduction of scarcity. It is a sad fact that much of what drives sales in the art world is scarcity, or how hard it is to get hold of one of your works. The reason that an artist's prices increase dramatically after they die is that it becomes a fact that there will never be any more of their work. Scarcity is important whether we like it or not for two reasons:

Firstly, if it is too easy to purchase your work, there is no immediacy. If you release a new set of prints every month, people will not feel compelled to buy one whilst they can, as they know more will be available soon, and so they are incentivised to wait until one that they can't resist catches their eye. As such, many wait so long that they forget, change their minds, or lose interest.

Secondly, it is another sad fact of the art world that a lot of collectors want their collection to be unique, as people don't often want something that *everyone* else has. The more works you put out there, the harder it is for you to control what is available when and where, as eventually buyers will become sellers via auctions and the secondary market. To many, art is an investment and a commodity. The less of your work there is available, the more people feel the need to buy a piece in the immediate present. Obviously don't underproduce either, however, as this can have the opposite effect. Make as many works as you feel compelled to, but it is important to not allow any old thing out of your studio.

2. DON'T RAISE YOUR PRICES TOO QUICKLY

We see a lot of artists make this mistake, and indeed we understand why they do. Being an artist is an expensive and unpredictable calling, and the prices of our works need to reflect that. It can be tempting for artists to taste a bit of success and raise their prices often and sharply, but this can be damaging for two reasons:

Firstly, you alienate a proportion of your existing buyers, as some of the people who collect your work now won't be able to afford your work with inflated prices. For this reason, it is much safer to slowly and incrementally increase your prices, never pricing-out a vast swathe of them all at once.

And secondly, as mentioned before, you run the risk of having to timidly lower your prices again after your sales dry up. This is sobering and turns collectors off your work.

It can be tempting to hike up your prices when you move to a new gallery or achieve another milestone on your to-do list, but many of your supporters will follow your career avidly and will notice these drastic changes in price. They will also notice the drops in price too, and so you want to avoid doing this at all costs. It makes your work look old and tired; another flavour of the month gone cold - and collectors care about this sort of thing.

A subcategory of this point is price consistency. Your prices should be the same regardless of whether you are selling the works through a gallery or direct from your studio. They should also be consistent whether you are working with a gallery that takes 30% or 50%. This is important for two reasons, firstly if someone buys direct from you and then later sees your work on sale in a gallery for 50% more, it looks like your prices have doubled overnight, and likewise, if this happens the other way around, it looks like you have had to drop your prices due to lack of sales. Secondly, if you are undercutting galleries by selling your works at half the price that they are, no collector is going to buy your work from a gallery, and in turn, no gallery is going to want to work with you.

3. DON'T STRESS TOO MUCH ABOUT CONSISTENCY VS EXPERIMENTATION

This is another question that we get asked a lot - should I find one thing that works and stick to it, or should I experiment wildly? If I experiment too much, how will all of my work be identifiably mine?

The answer to the first question is easy – no. There is nothing more uninteresting than an artist who flogs the same old dead horse over and over again, cashing in on something that has sold well in the past. This may do you well in the short-term, as people like to buy something that they recognise, but this soon becomes insipid and uninspiring. To quote Oscar Wilde – "Consistency is the last resort of the unimaginative." If you make something, people will know it's yours, and if they don't, then tell them.

Being wildly experimental might hurt your sales in the short term, but crassly churning out the same old work just because it sells well is easily noticeable, and turns people off in the long term. If you find one thing that works, don't do it to death, but don't abandon it either.

Experimentation is fun and exciting, and if you are having fun and are excited by your work, it is likely that your supporters will too.

If you avoid all of these commonly-occurring pitfalls and make work that is true to what you want it to do, eventually the sales should start happening organically. The important thing is to not try and force them when they aren't happening. We all go through dry periods, and one must have the stoic resolve not to change your approach or divert from your vision – just cut yourself some slack and keep making with yourself in mind. If you find yourself putting out less-exciting but more sellable works purely because they are more sellable, consider getting a part-time job to supplement your income instead. Not only can these pitfalls hamper your career progression in the short term, but they can have lasting effects that are hard to shake off.

PATRONS

As outlined earlier in this book, it's better to let the collectors come to you than for you to chase them. Assuming that they have come to you, it is a good idea to have an understanding of how and why people collect, and how it works when they interact with the artists from whom they purchase works. As we see it, there are three types of collector, all of which have different incentives and intentions when collecting.

INVESTMENT COLLECTORS

These are people with access to vast sums of money. These are often characterised as the 'serious' collectors, as they are the types to buy art for large sums of money to accompany their other high-value assets.

These collectors are sometimes incentivised to collect art as a way to store their money in a safe asset that can be sold if necessary. They are much more likely to be collecting for the prestige of owning something either so valuable, or so desirable, that others don't have. They aren't necessarily the type to flip artworks for a profit regularly, and are the type to bequeath art to either relatives or institutions upon their death. Often art sold to this type of collector is crated and stored in temperature-controlled warehouses, rather than hung upon walls.

These collectors don't necessarily pride themselves on their intimate knowledge of the art world to the same degree as the Mid-Level Collectors, and a lot of them actually work with advisors who select works for them, giving them more free time to engage in whatever other pursuits they have the energy for.

These collectors buy from art fairs and auctions, and as such have very little contact with the artists themselves, and so as artists selling your works, these aren't the type of collectors you should be expecting to court. When these collectors don't buy from auctions or fairs, they're usually purchasing from galleries.

MID-LEVEL COLLECTORS

The Mid-Level Collectors were once New Collectors (outlined below) and may become Investment Collectors later down the line. These collectors buy from galleries, but as they pride themselves on their deep understanding of the art world, they often want contact with the artists themselves too. These collectors engage with the art world in a more involved way than the New Collectors, and regularly attend openings and art fairs.

These collectors can be thought of as mavens, connecting and promoting artists simply by talking about them often to their similarly-art-savvy friends. These are the people that all artists and gallerists strive to attract, and they are the most exciting collectors to be around. They are likely to share your passion for art and collect out of a sincere love of it.

A subset of the Mid-Level Collectors are the Flippers, buying speculatively so that they can flip the works shortly afterwards for a profit. Rather than being collectors in the truest sense, the Flippers don't actually collect art – they trade in it, and as such do not warrant their own section here.

NEW COLLECTORS

The New Collectors are the easiest to attract, and so are the ones you will come into the closest-contact with early on in your career. These collectors may buy on a whim, or more specifically, on an emotion. They may find themselves drawn to an artwork and buy it, without necessarily doing research into the artist themselves. They have a modest level of disposable income and buy art because they like it. These collectors aren't necessarily interested in the art world to the same degree as the other types of collectors, but that doesn't mean that they never will be. Often these collectors become collectors because they see something that they like and will look good on a particular wall in their home, and this sparks an interest in art that becomes more substantial. They are obviously the most common types of art collectors, but many will dip in and out of art collection naturally, and for some, their collection is complete with a single piece. This means that you may sell one work to someone and then not hear from them for years, but keep them on your mailing list until they ask to be removed, as you never know when they will be ready to add another work to their collection.

Art is essentially a luxury product, and as such, whilst people may *feel* the need to buy, this isn't from an immediate and actual need, but a want. When dealing with collectors, you must strive to understand their needs, and in turn, aim to accommodate them as much as is possible. Selling an artwork should not be seen as merely a transaction; a means to an end in attaining money, but as a mutually-beneficial agreement. Your collectors are essential in maintaining your practice if you need to sell works to survive, but this should be a pleasant experience for both parties. You should get to know your collectors, as the most likely people to buy one of your new works, are those who have bought from you in the past.

The most important thing is always to respect your collectors. The sale of an artwork should benefit each party as much as it does the other, and so rather than thinking only of what you can get from someone, also try to think about what you can contribute to make their lives happier too. Having a dedicated group of collectors who are interested in your work is an invaluable resource, and as such, they should be treated with the requisite amount of respect, and humility.

PLAYING TO THE COLLECTORS

Art collectors are a major driving force in the success of many artists' careers. For better or worse, the sale of works is what gives them validation.

Sales should not be the only factor in determining someone's success (or lack thereof), but to some, a strong sales record is all that matters. We believe this approach to evaluate success can be damaging, as success is subjective and flexible. That being said, artists need to sell their works to facilitate the buying of more materials and the creation of space in which to make new works.

Collectors are often seen cynically as advancing the commodification of the art world. The trend for buying low and selling high, flipping works for a profit and buying as an investment has tarred an otherwise very supportive and genuine process that is done with the best of intentions by the vast majority of collectors.

This is sadly something that does a disservice to people who have a genuine, passionate love for art, and who use their resources to support the artists they love.

In the writing of this book, we spoke to numerous dedicated collectors and were struck by their sincere love for artists and the art they produce. Not one of the collectors we spoke to cited the re-saleability of the works, or the trajectory of an artist's career being driving factors in how they selected works.

Claus Busch Risvig was the first collector we spoke to and we were struck by the continued support that he invests in the artists he collects. He is engaged in the art world to a much more involved level than someone simply looking to make a quick profit off the back of a shrewd investment.

Of the questions asked of this sample group of collectors, one thing that they all made a point of mentioning is that for them to decide to buy a piece, they had to have a strong, intense emotional connection to the work right from the very beginning. It was only after this reaction that they would research details about the artist and their career; the heart leads and the brain follows.

"The whole process starts with a feeling. How does the work make us feel? Does it stick in our minds? Does it challenge us? If so, we start to dive deeper into the work and its creator." Claus Busch Risvig

"What can an artist do to make their work more collectible?" we asked, playing devil's advocate for a moment. Overwhelmingly their response was simple: don't.

The artists that make work to sell, and dilute the meaning of their work with sales in mind, may do well in the short-term, but this success will be short-lived and transparent. What must come first is the honesty and integrity of an artist's work, for it to even reach a point at which cynical ploys to 'strike while the iron is hot' are even possible.

It is true that some artists who achieve monumental success early on in their careers seem to churn out work without it harming the desirability of their output, but this can only happen after they have achieved their initial success.

True collectors, of art rather than of commodities, want to see a real passion for creation from artists that they collect - an intense need to create that defines their existence.

We have heard of artists finding and contacting collectors on things like LinkedIn and Instagram, but ultimately this is the job of the gallery/dealer, not the artist. When an artist is seen to be doing things like this it can seem at best: a little pushy, and at worst: desperate. This may work some of the time, but we - and the collectors we have spoken to – wouldn't advise it as an approach.

To conclude upon how artists can appeal to collectors, we would simply say this: don't go out of your way to try to make this happen.

That isn't a glass-half-empty statement, rather an avowal that if you are creating for the right reasons, and there is an integrity and a well-thought-out methodology of why you are doing what it is you are doing, eventually, the collectors will come find you.

"Keep working hard, believe in the work you do, and don't be afraid to experiment and make mistakes."
Claus Busch Risvig

THE IMPORTANCE OF COLLABORATION

Ellie Pennick

with Alex Newell

Privileged institutions with financial and cultural capital need to confront the major lack of resources available to systematically disadvantaged artists, and help facilitate their success. The dog-eat-dog mindset plaguing the art world stifles talent and breeds rivalries.

How can grassroots galleries challenge the system? We have a platform and we need to use it. It won't be easy, but a progressive network of galleries offering support for artists to advance their careers is where we can start. At Guts, we see other galleries as our collaborators, not our competitors, and we've been working with other gallerists to oppose the current gallery business model.

Gallery outreach is often localised, which can create artificial borders. Collaboration between independent galleries can expand geographical involvement to collectors, consumers, and communities nationwide.

WHAT CAN WE ACHIEVE BY WORKING TOGETHER?

We can share physical spaces to counter the rent crisis so that gallerists that can't find or afford a permanent space can still contribute to the evolving art scene. This also allows gallery directors to experiment with different, unusual spaces and appeal to various audiences across the country so that they're not limited by the footfall in the vicinity of their permanent space.

We can share ideas and innovate together. Artists, art collectors, and art directors are passionate about the same thing. We can harness that energy to swap contacts and bounce off one another to better our outcomes.

Let's breed talent by placing artists in new spaces with wider audiences. This can only improve circumstances for struggling artists by raising the profile of their work. We can share collector contacts to increase selling prospects for artists and bring in investment opportunities for gallerists.

In an increasingly solipsistic society, bridging cultural barriers presents opportunities to fight bigotry. We want to promote underprivileged artists from oppressed groups. We want to promote the creative observations of society at large through the medium of art. And we want to earn a decent living for the valuable work we do.

WHAT DO YOU WISH ALL ARTISTS DID MORE OR LESS?

GALERIE CHLOE SALGADO

Self-promotion (both more and less depending on the artist)

STEINSLAND BERLINER

More work in the studio/less stress

PUBLIC GALLERY

Collaborate more (not just artists but galleries too)

WILLIAM GUSTAFSSON OF UNION GALLERY

To not be afraid of discounts as it's about getting your work out there

PIERMARQ ART

Less comparing yourselves to others, please!

JEANETTE GUNNARSSON OF KRISTIAN DAY GALLERY

Less: Worry about Instagram. It's easy to get caught up in social media, but good art takes time and lots of it, put the art first all else will follow. More: Look at art, study it, think about it – continuously, constantly, obsessively

MAKING TRENDS

An Interview with Paul Foster

Curator at the Saatchi Gallery

D What advice would you give to an emerging artist that is looking to get their work noticed?

PF Do not compromise on the work. Keep producing strong work, keep developing your thinking and your techniques. Put in place measures to communicate and present this artwork simply and effectively but without this activity becoming too distracting or time-consuming. Have a website or presence online that makes it very easy for anyone who sees a social media post to find the greater body of your work and access it easily. When that gallerist, curator or buyer sees an image, you do not want to lose their interest because they cannot find your work or contact details online, right there and then.

D How do you think social media has affected the life of an emerging artist - has it made it easier or harder to 'be visible'?

PF It has made it easier for more work by more artists to be seen momentarily, and often as part of a stream of small digital images. Social media makes it harder for works to be considered meaningfully, or as the artist might wish them to be perceived. Visibility is fleeting but that is the arena in which images compete for attention, and a fraction of the views may lead to positive developments.

D Do you think that social media has necessitated a change in the traditional artist/gallery relationship?

PF Not fundamentally. The underlying principles of the promotion of the artist and gallery, the building of reputations, and the return on investment for each party are the same. However, social media has provided artists with a route to buyers and viewers that bypass any gallery. For artists that make a success of social media, it strengthens their position and reduces any dependence upon galleries.

From a gallery perspective, if an artist can demonstrate a large and engaged following on social media then this indicates a potential market for the work of the artist. Artists and galleries should seek to develop and build an audience via all channels, but the weighting should vary from artist to artist.

D In general, do you think early-career artists face more pressure these days?

PF No, but the nature of the pressure has changed. What is true now also applies to the past, namely: artists struggle in anonymity to get recognition, with very few opportunities to be noticed. In the past, this was due to a scarcity of opportunities, the few channels open to them, and the narrow (and closed) nature of those channels. Now the struggle is that each artist exists as a drop in an ocean of artists all competing for the attention of a fickle audience consuming an unprecedented number of images daily. The failure rate for artists has probably not changed very much – it is still very, very high.

D By what measure should emerging artists quantify success or career progression?

PF 1. Happiness , 2. Recognition, 3. Positive engagement from an audience, 4. Reward.

D Speaking as a curator, what would be the one thing that you wish artists would do more, or be better at?

PF Understand that the most successful artists combine a high quality of thought and or emotion with a high quality of execution. Work hard on developing your prowess on all these elements.

D And what is something you would like to see artists doing less?

PF Too many artists seek to find a magic recipe for works that sell. The results can be a patchwork of icons or be derivative and without anything original to say. Seek to make trends – not follow them.

COURSE-CORRECTING

When undertaking a career that is composed of self-authored initiatives, it is common to feel as if you might not be heading in the right direction. This can be intimidating, but it is also exciting to get lost once in a while, for this is where we make discoveries.

Being an artist relies upon a great deal of creativity, motivation, and experimentation. When artists undertake this experimentation, they often hit a dead-end, run out of steam, or change their minds about what their intentions are. Once they reach one of these natural conclusions, it can be hard to identify them as such, and so artists often continue ploughing on despite their waning interest and inspiration.

If we have spent a considerable amount of time pursuing one particular goal, it can be hard to abandon it even if we want to. This is called the Sunk-Cost Fallacy and causes people to waste extra time, money, and effort on something when they don't actually value the potential outcome as much as they did when they started. If indeed we do reach the point at which we realise that this course of action is a dead-end, we worry too much about the time we have already spent on the project and think that were we to abandon it now, that time would be wasted. That time is already lost whether you continue or not, and as such, when deciding whether or not to press on, you should consider how much time you would save by abandoning this failed course of action.

If artists were to follow through to completion of every idea they had, they wouldn't make half the amount of breakthroughs that they do.

Abandoning a project or work that has become a chore is often incredibly freeing and allows you to draw a line under it and move on, utilising the saved time to work on something more productive.

If you are having to force yourself to continue with something you aren't enjoying, it is never going to be your best work.

The things we create have a life of their own once we've let them out of the studio, so it's best to limit the amount of ones that we aren't happy with.

PEAKS AND TROUGHS

The life of an artist is a difficult one. Sadly, there is a trend for subterfuge around this issue, as every artist wants to appear to be as successful as possible, so as to not spook their collectors and galleries. As much as some may protest otherwise, the image presented to the world is but a facade: a clever mask concealing all of our worries, struggles, and failures. This is dangerous in two ways: firstly, struggling in silence is struggling alone, and the inability to share these struggles with the world forces us to face them in secret. Secondly, it gives the impression to everyone else struggling in silence that they are the only ones not selling out shows and fighting off collectors.

In the research for this book, we have spoken to countless artists about the everyday battles they face, in the hope that this pulling-back of the curtain allows others to realise that these hardships are widespread and universal, regardless of what level of career one may be at.

Money is by far the greatest concern for many artists, as the unpredictable nature of selling work forces people to budget and save for the months when sales are slower than others. Before a big show can be a particularly trying time, as the majority of your output is kept under-wraps, unsellable until the private view. Artists spend months and sometimes years working for shows, and thus are often unable to attend to much else – including making money to pay the bills.

Many artists supplement their income via employment, either within the art world or outside of it. Prominent artists such as Andrea Fraser, Chris Burden, Michael Craig Martin, and Bas Jan Ader were/are lecturers and teachers at arts universities. Damien Hirst was once a gallery assistant, and Jeff Koons worked on the membership desk at MoMa. The list goes on.

Some artists choose to continue these jobs long after they have 'made it'. Minimalist composer Phillip Glass was a plumber, and once found himself installing the dishwasher of Time Magazine's art critic Robert Hughes. He also started his own removal business with Chuck Close and Richard Serra. Sarah Lucas, at the height of the YBA fame, decided to get a one-day-a-week job as a barmaid.

Another thing that artists struggle with is the constant and inevitable ebb-and-flow of popularity. Even the most successful artists swing in and out of the limelight at times, and it's unlikely that people will always be clamouring for your work. One body of work might not resonate with the public in the same that the previous one did. These things happen: move on and get working on the next series.

The art world is also, *still*, sadly too focused on what is and isn't fashionable at any given time, and as an artist whose work just isn't of the style that's 'in', it's hard not to get disheartened when you see people falling over themselves trying to get hold of what to you are unexciting works. It's hard not to attempt to cater to the hysteria, to alter your practice to fit in with what's in demand, but you should remain steadfast in your refusal to do so. What is in now, may not be in a year or two. While this may seem like a problem for only the emerging artist, it is often the more established ones who worry (secretly) about not being relevant. To have been relevant at one point, and to worry that time has gone, can be terrifying. We know artists who have had sell-out shows who still worry about this kind of thing, so believe us when we say it is widespread.

Self-doubt is widespread and inevitable, as artists are perfectionists. To create something is to reflect upon it, and to reflect upon your own work is to critique it. All artists face this delicate balance of equilibrium on a daily basis. No artist would develop if they weren't continually evaluating their past work and considering how they could have done it better, or what they would have done differently were they to be doing that same piece now. It is imperative to question our past work, as to do so is to learn lessons in order to progress in the future. And it's why it's incredibly common for an artist to fluctuate in between the rigid self-belief that such a job requires, and crushing self-doubt. The arts industry is based partially upon the public image of the artist, and often these struggles are faced in private. To admit that you worry about how your work is being received by the public is widely-believed to appear to doubt yourself, and if you are doubting yourself, how can anyone else be expected to believe in you. This is a misleading, and ultimately destructive mentality, and one that we can only break by admitting that all artists, including ourselves, still face the very same struggles no matter what level of career they are at.

When you create something as personal as an artwork, it takes a lot of courage to present it to the world. For this to then not be met with universal praise can knock your resolve and test your confidence. Rest assured, however, that even the most successful artists still feel upset when what they believe to be great work isn't lauded as such by the public.

The trials of being an artist are real, and as well as celebrating our successes, we must acknowledge, and learn from our hardships. If something that you do is met with dislike or ambivalence do not worry – for you are not alone. Furthermore, it is only indifference we should fear.

IN PURSUIT OF BEING AN ARTIST

Hedley Roberts

My experience as an artist and educator tells me that good art education is a balance of three main components; firstly the creative development, then theoretical socio-political-historical-philosophical context, and then the professional 'business' of being an artist. As time has gone on, the focus of UK art education has changed from being mainly about the development of creativity and the 'subject', to an increased focus on graduate readiness for their chosen industry. This change was precipitated by an increase of access to education and an ideological paradigm shift that introduced student loans and the student fees system. As a result, there is more focus on what knowledge and skills a graduate needs than ever before. As the head of an art school, I now make sure we have lectures from intellectual property specialists, accountants, marketing professionals, and social media experts, as well as from recent graduates, established creatives and theorists from a wide range of backgrounds. Of course, not every artist goes to art school for their education, and these components can be developed without being in a classroom or art school. In my own network, I'm increasingly connecting with successful artists that have made it without any formal art education. They've gained business knowledge from other sectors, from friends, or by making mistakes and learning from it. What follows here is some of the advice that will help you whether you go to art school or you find another way.

Ok, so before we start looking at some of the basics, we need to talk about the art world. The A-list art world is brutal, unregulated, narcissistic, and subject to lots of nefarious business practices – because a lot of money can change hands. A-list artists, galleries and dealers get most of the press, but they're more like big corporate brands and their behaviours and measures of success are similar to big business. But the A-list is only one world, and there are many others; museum artists, popular artists, community artists, residency artists, public art, civic art, and many more. The truth is that there are many artists that aren't celebrated that are making a very good living in lots of different ways, and there are critically acclaimed artists that subsidise a lack of sales income with other means. There are also plenty of artists who have financial resources and privilege at their disposal to help them gain success. It's not a level playing field, and it's important to acknowledge that. To be successful, you need to think about what kind of art you want to make, what kind of artist you want to be, and what success looks like for you. For example, is it achieving a degree, or getting an exhibition in a major museum and a place in history, or is it just making a living from your art? The most obvious route is graduating, having exhibitions, making sales, and getting critical recognition. The most important strategy is to set up a supportive sustainable strategic plan that will be there for you when the going gets tough because the truth is that the art world is challenging to navigate. You might get success straight out of art school or you might have your first solo exhibition in your 60s. Along the way, you might have a myriad of different jobs, successes, and disappointments. Your career will rise and fall, and rise again – but only if you are able to maintain the tenacity required to continue making art when no galleries seem interested, and there are no sales.

Firstly, if you want to be an artist, make art. Then make more art. When you've made that art, make another kind of art. When you're not making art, talk about art. If there's nobody to talk to, write about art and read about art. There's no other route to developing good art than making, and learning about, as much of it as you can.

Perhaps the most important piece of advice is to document your work. Start doing this from day one and keep doing it. Make it part of your regular practice. Don't wait to be told when and how to do it, and don't wait until the work is 'good'. There are lots of online resources on how to do this. Make sure the images are clear and sharp, and that the lighting is good. Keep visual notes of technical processes, colour palettes, work in progress, and your studio. These images will be a resource for the future. Organise your documentation into folders on an online resource like Dropbox. I'd advise getting into the habit of making an inventory of works that you make using spreadsheet software like Google Sheets. You can use the rows and columns to list the works, media, and sizes. As you set up your business, you can use it to list prices, available works, location of the works on loan, and who bought what.

The next is to manage and monitor your finances. Nobody likes doing this, but if you get into the habit early on, it'll be easier in the future. You'll spend money on materials, subsistence, glasses, studio clothes, books, travel, studio rent, marketing, social media, internet, mobile phone bills, software for your phone, van hire, storage, fabrication, and framing, etc. You'll need to understand what you are spending so you can understand what you're investing, and this will eventually help you to understand your pricing and your business. Most of what you spend on your art will be tax-deductible and the art that you make will become your 'stock' and will have a value. When you sell your first work you'll need to complete a tax return, and if you have records and receipts it'll be easier. It's likely that your business as an artist will make a loss at the beginning because your outgoings will exceed your sales.

As you begin to establish your creative practice, you need to start reflecting on it and writing about it. I believe that making and reflecting are two different processes. The creative making phase often requires you to be in the flow of the moment, when that's over you stand back and look at what you're doing and then think about it. It's at this moment that you need to start to think about how to write about what you're doing. Words are useful tools to explain visual things to people who are more used to interpreting things through words, so you need to get used to articulating your ideas this way too. Keep a journal where you write about anything that interests you. There's no wrong way to do this, but it needs to be done. A good way to learn how to do it is to read the writing of other artists that you like in their press releases, statements, and biographies. But also watch them being interviewed talking about their work. They'll have developed a language and have regular words and phrases that they use. Make a note of these, and use them if they're relevant to you. In the future, you'll be asked to present or talk about your work. If you've spent time writing to yourself about it, you'll have reflected on your ideas and spent time editing and selecting the ones that are important to you. This is also the best way to begin writing artists statements.

Art is principally about ideas, so find out about as many ideas as you can. These don't have to be 'art' ideas (but these are useful too). Art making is about 'being in the world', and the world is an infinite resource that you can use to develop your subject and interests that can then be put into your art. Science, philosophy, gardening, cookery, politics, engineering, astrology, medicine – it's all research material that artists make work about. There will be a library somewhere near you, and you should try to put aside time to go there. There's an infinite amount of resources online, but the library is a sanctuary for research. If you don't read because you're dyslexic, there are lots of video interviews, podcasts, and audiobooks. Put them on headphones and listen in the studio. Take notes on anything that you think is important to you.

Artists often work alone in the studio, but they're always part of a network and an ecology. One of the ways I help my students focus on this is to ask them to pick 10 contemporary artists that they would like to be in an exhibition with. The artist has to be alive and just slightly above them in the spectrum of being 'established'. They have to then read and research the artists, finding out everything about them – their biography and backstory, where they went to school, what exhibitions they were in, artists they exhibited with, galleries they exhibited in, awards they won. They need to read the artists' statements, press releases, and articles written about them. They need to note key words, phrases, relationships. They then have to create a 'synaptic diagram' with images, words, and links between all the elements. They then use this to create a file which organises all the information. This is a very strategic approach to knowing and understanding how your particular art world is connected. This exercise can be undertaken at whatever stage you're at in your art career. As you become established and experienced, it becomes integrated into your professional existence, but it's always good to do as an evaluative exercise.

Artists have to write about their work or persuade someone else to do it for them. Even then, they need to be able to articulate their ideas to the person writing. There is a lot of criticism of the artist statement. Often art schools encourage students to make grand claims for their work, and the reason for this is that the art school is trying to encourage the student to be as ambitious as possible; to imagine themselves as a successful A-list artist. This is a good idea but can make student art statements sound naive or overblown and pompous. Thankfully this trend is slowing. If you've been writing in your journal, you'll have focused your thoughts about your work. Try to write simply and clearly in your own words about your work. If in doubt keep to the subject, media, and core idea. Write about things in the world that interest you and how these connect into your work; for example science, medicine, or politics. Don't quote dense art-theory or other artists unless it's absolutely essential to the concept of your practice.

'Continuing Professional Development' or CPD is a term used in human resources management. It basically identifies the strategic objectives and activities that an individual needs to undertake to continue to be viable and improve their career in the workplace. If you think about your art as a business then you need to undertake 'continuing professional development'. Doing a degree in art to become an artist is a kind of professional development. Attending artist development workshops run at your regional gallery is also, as is reading an article online about how to improve your social media reach, or getting some inside information from a friend about a gallery to work with. My point is, that both we as individuals and the professional world we work in, are continually changing. So we need to understand that learning is lifelong and continuous. CPD is best when it's documented and reflected on annually as part of a plan in your career journey. If you want to be able to measure your achievement, you need to be able to understand where you started out from, what your intentions were, where you planned to go, and how you planned to get there. Along the way, plans change and that's ok, but then the plan needs to be re-evaluated and you need to reconsider your intention. Try to outline a plan for one year, five years, and ten years. Set objectives for each of these and make them challenging but measurable. For example; "year one: a group exhibition at a regional gallery, and an application to a funding body", then think about how you will achieve that. Do you need CPD to get more knowledge or skills to help you achieve that? Do the same for five years, and ten years. Be ambitious, but be reasonable. Try to slightly over-achieve, because it's good for your self-worth.

So, you know what kind of artist you want to be and you've documented and written about your work. Your creative art practice is developing, you've had a couple of exhibitions, and maybe some sales. You've attended some classes with a local artists development agenda and written your first funding bid, but it was unsuccessful and you've got nothing in the pipeline for next year. What are you missing? The answer is community. This is the most important and least documented aspect of any successful artists development – an ability to develop a supportive community. A collective of artists who actively work together to support each other is the holy grail of artist strategies. All artists need this, and the sooner you begin to establish quality connections and networks with other artists that you can relate to, the better. As you develop you will help each other. This is what gallery openings are about, and what social media is best used for. You'll recommend each other to galleries, curators, collectors, and editors. You'll develop an agenda and an energy between yourselves and that will help you maintain your mental health. The best collectives are fluid and without definition. Some will leave and new artists will join. You'll share knowledge and inside information, you'll promote each other.

Ultimately, your success will depend entirely on the strength and quality of your network. No artist does it alone.

WHAT IS THE ONE BIT OF ADVICE YOU WOULD GIVE AN ARTIST AT THE START OF THEIR CAREER?

RICHARD STONE

I can't recall who said it, but it was something like, remember, you're a good artist at 40, a great artist at 50. I'm not saying that artists don't make really strong work early on, but I think there's something honest about how much you have to grow and how resilient you need to be

ANDY DIXON

You won't get respect for work you haven't done yet. Put in the work first and everything else will come later

TOM ANHOLT
Work harder than you think you need to and be a nice person

ERIN LAWLOR
Be curious and work hard

ANDREW SALGADO
Work twice as hard and worry half as much. Don't expect too much too soon: it's a marathon, not a sprint, and too much attention too early can actually turn out to harm your career in the long-run

LUKE HANNAM
Don't settle on a style too quickly, even if it gets you attention

JENNY BROSINSKI

Be yourself

HEDLEY ROBERTS

Being an artist is a long term project, keep going no matter what. If you're still making work when you've been rejected, when there are no sales, and there are no exhibition opportunities; if you're working other jobs to support your artwork, if you keep going no matter what... then you're a successful artist

NEVA HOSKING

Paid dues don't pay rent, don't let people take advantage of you. I used to be so flattered people liked my work that I let them walk all over me; I'm still learning

JUSTIN LEE WILLIAMS

To take every artist that gives you advice and understand it's just advice, and there is no right or wrong way to approach being an artist. Also to not be so hard on yourself, the work you are making now will not at all be the same work you produce 10 or 20 years into the future, so let it go and learn fast

FIONA GRADY

To enjoy their practice! You can tell when an artist is engaged and excited by what they are doing. There's a lot of pressure on young artists to be 'discovered' but takes time and hard work to develop your career

CATHERINE HAGGARTY

Be very active and generous to the artists around you. Keep your overheads very low and make work all the time with no concern of showing or selling. It's a marathon!

RAE HICKS

Don't believe a word anyone says. Almost everything – proclamations, snide digs, hubris, advice, and eulogising – is nonsense. Absolutely no one has the faintest idea what the fuck is going on

AFTERWORD

In the writing of this book, there were a lot of topics that we wanted to address, but sadly we weren't able to include everything. We hope that what we have covered has been useful, even if its use is that it has aided you in identifying what it is that you don't want to do. What is important for us is attempting to aid emerging-artists in any way that we can, whilst also acknowledging that we are not infallible. Some of what you read here might not apply to your particular experience, and that's ok. There is no sure-fire road to success in this world, and so, unfortunately, there is no winning formula that once applied guarantees success. Hopefully though, through the course of reading this book, you have discovered some ideas or perspectives that you hadn't thought of before.

To link up with us in the digital world, we can be found here:

delphiangallery.com
info@delphiangallery.com
@delphiangallery
facebook.com/delphiangallery

THANKS

Firstly, thanks to Daniel Fletcher and Foolscap Editions for their amazing support in helping us to produce and release this book. Special thanks to William Lyall for all his design work.

Thanks to all at theprintspace for the support you have given to Delphian from day one, and for your continued belief in the ethos of Delphian.

Thanks to all of the artists, curators, and writers that we have worked with since we launched, and thanks to everyone who has ever come to one of our shows, bought work, or said kind things about us online.

And an especially large thank you to all of the people we interviewed for the book. Please, everyone, check out their work and support them in any way you can.

Thank you to every artist we have worked with, you are the reason that we do what we do.

Thank you to the writers who contributed one of the guest essays: Rosalind Davis, Paul Weiner, Jordy Kerwick, Hector Campbell, Ellie Pennick, Paul Foster, Hedley Roberts.

Thanks also to: Sarah Forman, Jacob Barnes, Stuart Waplington, Wingshan Smith, Oona Vaisanen, Jen Lloyd, George Stuart-Lockhart, Alex Newell, Katherine Kluznik, Hilary Thompson, Paul Thompson, Frances Murphy, Geraldine Murphy, and Euphrosyne Andrews.

FURTHER READING

ART/WORK: EVERYTHING YOU NEED TO KNOW (AND DO) AS YOU PURSUE YOUR ART CAREER - HEATHER DARCY BHANDARI

This book is comprehensive and informative, containing everything from detailed diagrams of how to crate your paintings, to instructions on hanging and insuring your works. An irreplaceable toolkit essential to all early-career artists.

WHAT THEY DIDN'T TEACH YOU IN ART SCHOOL: WHAT YOU NEED TO KNOW TO SURVIVE AS AN ARTIST - ROSALIND DAVIS AND ANNABEL TILLEY

Rosalind Davis also wrote a short essay for this book, for which we are eternally grateful. She has also participated in panel-discussions with us, and has spent a lot of her career supporting, and educating early-career artists. This book from her and Annabel is another essential for all artists.

HOW TO WRITE ABOUT CONTEMPORARY ART - GILDA WILLIAMS

Writing about their own work is something that all artists struggle with early on in their careers. This is understandable, but also fixable. This book is an incredible resource that will help you write everything from artist statements to press releases and everything in between.

SELLING ART ONLINE, AND HOW TO SHOW YOUR WORK - CREATIVEHUB

Creativehub have produced these two incredible books, which we would definitely recommend. They are the leaders in their field, as well as being involved in all areas of the arts.

THE CURATOR'S HANDBOOK: MUSEUMS, COMMERCIAL GALLERIES, INDEPENDENT SPACES – ADRIEN GEORGE

Having an understanding of all aspects of what it takes to host an exhibition is important for all artists, not just artist-curators. Knowing what it's like on the other side will benefit you greatly, and if that is your aim, this book is essential.

FOOLSCAP EDITIONS

Foolscap Editions is an independent publisher founded in 2016 that works in close collaboration with artists to release books and special editions. Foolscap Editions supported Delphian in the production of this book.

foolscap-editions.com
info@foolscap-editions.com
@foolscap.editions

2ND EDITION

PUBLISHED
July 2020

DESIGN
William Lyall

PRINTING
Kopa

ISBN
978-1-9997990-4-5

delphiangallery.com
foolscap-editions.com